TIN CAN
PAPERMAKING
Recycle for Earth and Art

by
Arnold E. Grummer

Greg Markim, Incorporated
Publishers, Appleton, Wisconsin 54912

1992

Dedicated to my favorite people, Mabe, Mark, Greg, Kim, Dave, Jon, Dan, and Ellie, for any one of whom I would give up even tin can papermaking.

Grummer, Arnold E.
    Tin can papermaking : recycle for earth and art / by Arnold E. Grummer
    p. cm.
    Preassigned LCCN: 92-121267.
    ISBN 0-938251-01-5

    1. Waste paper–Recycling. 2. Papermaking. 3. Paper, Handmade.
  I. Title.

TS1120.5.G7 1992   676'.22
                                    QBI92-1440

Greg Markim, Inc.
PO Box 13245, Milwaukee, WI 53213

Printed in the United States of America
Grummer, Arnold E. 1923 -

Printing History: Second Printing, December 1992

Summary: Step-by-step directions for recycling paper into new handmade decorative and art sheets, using a blender and tin cans, and other materials found around the kitchen.

ISBN 0-938251-01-5

Thanks to all the scientists and technicians at the former Institute of Paper Chemistry in Appleton, WI who introduced me to the wonders and the facts of paper and the amazing fibers that make it up.

Acknowledgements

INTRODUCTION

Can you *really* recycle waste paper into beautiful
new art or decorative paper?
Can you *really* make good paper with two tin
cans?

The answer to both questions is "yes!" Easily.
That's what this book is about. But now, move
into action — set the stage for making your own
paper *by* recycling and *with* two tin cans.

Table of Contents

TIN CAN PAPERMAKING

RECYCLING FOR EARTH

Chapter One

Gather the "Easy Eight"

(If you have purchased this book with a Tin Can Papermaking™ Kit, you already have all necessary materials. Proceed to making paper by directions in the following chapter or the direction sheet and materials in the papermaking kit.)

To make tin can paper, you need eight items. Six are probably already in your home.

1. Tin Cans

Get two. Twenty-six ounce coffee cans are great. Other tin cans will work. The size (diameter) of the cans will determine the size of your paper.

Cut one end out of one can. Cut both ends out of the other.

2. Support Screen

Since this screen supports the papermaking screen, it needs to be quite rigid. Hardware cloth is excellent. It is sufficiently rigid. Like window screen, it has strands going in both directions, but the strands and the opening between them are both bigger. Hardware cloth is sold at hardware stores. It often comes in three different sizes of openings (mesh). Any of the sizes works. You need at least a 6x6-inch piece. Get a little extra.

3. Papermaking Screen

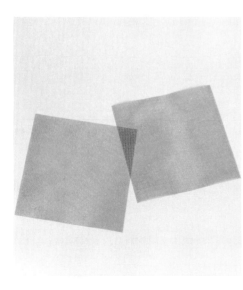

Get non-metal (for safety) window screen. A minimum of two 6x6-inch pieces are needed. Get a little extra. Window screen is right on the edge of being too coarse for papermaking, but most of the time it will work alright. Later you might want to experiment with other "sieves" such as cloth, etc..

4. Sponge

Sponges are a natural for water removal. Get a good cellulose sponge not too big or too little for your hand. A 6 3/8 x 3 5/8 x 1-inch is good. Get one that is good for soaking up water.

5. Paper Towels

Get large size paper towels, singles or in a roll. (Kit uses reuseable couch sheets). As said elsewhere, after paper towels (couch sheets) get wet from being used, they are dried and reused. Don't throw them away—handle with care.

6. Board for Pressing

This will be used to press down on a wet sheet between layers of towels. Use a size that fits your hand. One near 6 inches long by 3 or 4 inches wide is nice. Anything similar to a board, such as a book (in plastic to keep it from getting damp) can be used.

7. Clothes Iron

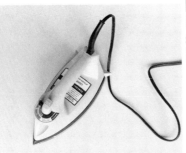

Paper wanted right away must be dried by heat. Heat can be supplied by your iron turned to its highest setting.

BE SURE THE STEAM IS TURNED OFF!

8. Blender

Any kitchen blender will do. Some brands are better than others. If buying new, get a model with the fewest speeds. They work as well and are less expensive. When you have the above, the stage is set. Now — on to actual recycling of old paper into new.

Chapter Two

Step-By-Step
Recycling and Papermaking

Step 1.

Get a tin can with one end cut out. Set it on a level surface, open-end up.

Step 2.

Over the tin can's open end, place a 6 x 6-inch piece of hardware cloth.

Step 3.

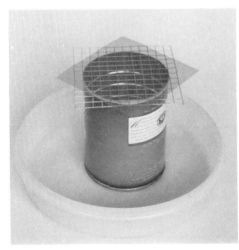

Place a 6 x 6-inch piece of non-metal window screen on top of the hardware cloth.

Step 4.

Place a tin can with both ends cut out over the window screen. If the cans are of the same size, match their rims. (The top can can be smaller, but not larger, than the bottom can.) Presto! You have set up a "pour" hand mold with which you can make handmade paper.

Step 5.

Pick a piece of 7 x 7-inch waste or used paper, or smaller pieces of several papers which in total add up to about 7 x 7 inches.

Step 6.

Tear up the paper into small pieces. Put the pieces into a blender. Add about one and a half cups of water.

Step 7. **PUT ON THE LID!**

Step 8. Run the blender for about 20 to 30 seconds.

Step 9.

Pour half the blender's contents into each of two containers.

Step 10.

Add about a half-cup water to each container.

Step 11.

Take one container in each hand. Pour rapidly (not slowly, but *dump*) contents of both containers at the same time, into the top can. Pour from opposite sides so that streams from the two containers hit each other.

Note: **Pouring can also be done with one hand. Pour your pulp into one container. Add water. Hold the top can down with one hand. Pour with the other.**

Step 12. Let all water drain into the bottom can.

Step 13.

Raise the top can straight up and off. ***THERE ON THE WINDOW SCREEN IS YOUR NEW SHEET.***

Step 14. Lift the new sheet and window screen off the support screen. Place them on a flat surface not harmed by water (table top, several layers of cloth, piece of plastic, etc.).

Step 15. Place another 6 x 6-inch piece of window screen over the new sheet (for protection).

Step 16.

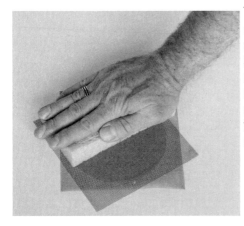

Take a sponge and press it down on top of the window screen and new sheet. Squeeze water from the sponge. Continue pressing and squeezing until the entire sheet has been covered and the sponge removes little, or no more, water.

Step 17.

Carefully start at one corner and peel off the top window screen.

Step 18. Lay down three folded paper towels on top of each other.

Note: **When folded, towels must still be wider than the new sheet. If not, get bigger towels, or don't fold.**

Step 19.

Pick up the screen with the new sheet on it. Turn them over onto the towels, new sheet against top towel.

Step 20. Apply sponge as before *(Step 16)*. This time push down with as much force as possible. Apply pressure over entire new sheet.

Note: **Pressure applied here will cause new sheet to stay with the towels when the screen is peeled off. That is why a lot of pressure is needed.**

Step 21. Starting slowly at one corner, peel off the window screen, leaving the new sheet on the towels. If the sheet rises with the screen, apply the sponge again with all the force you can. If the sheet still rises with the screen, carefully peel a corner of the new sheet from the screen, and separate the two with care. At the end of this step, the new sheet should be on top of the paper towels.

Step 22.

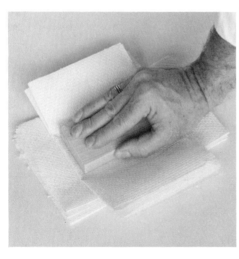

Fold three more paper towels. Place them on top of the new sheet. Take a flat piece of wood, or other flat item, and press down hard on top of the dry towels.

Step 23. Remove the top wet towels. Replace with dry ones. Repeat pressing. Repeat replacement of wet towels with dry ones, and pressing, until little water is removed with dry towels.

Note: When the new sheet has become strong enough in above step, lift it off wet towels beneath it. Replace the wet towels with dry ones. The idea is to get as much water out of the new sheet as possible.

Note: Do not throw wet towels away. Lay them out to dry. *Re-use them in future papermaking.*

Step 24. Put the new sheet on an ironing board or other dry, clean surface that will not be harmed by heat. Turn clothes iron to top heat. Iron new sheet dry. Move iron slowly but steadily so that all parts of sheet dry at about the same rate.

Note: Placing a thin cloth over the sheet for ironing is wise. It protects the iron's surface from possible heat-sticky additives that might have been in paper that was recycled.

Step 25. When the sheet is dry, shout, yell, wave arms, sing the National Anthem (but not like you-know-who), call neighbors over, and call reporters and photographers from local newspaper, radio and TV stations. You are an artist and an environmentalist.

You have—*for earth and art*—RECYCLED!

Four Art and Decorative Techniques and the Pulp Gun

RECYCLING FOR ART

Chapter Three

Mottled Surface Technique

Discussion. Run long enough, the blender will reduce paper to individual fibers.

But, the blender can be turned off before all the paper comes apart. This would leave many small paper "chunks" in the resulting pulp. If the paper being recycled were parts of sheets of several different colors, or of a single sheet on which there were many different ink colors, the "chunks" could be of many different colors. When a sheet is formed with the pulp, the many individual fibers sink to the screen while the "colored chunks" tend to float to the surface. This can result in surfaces that are very interesting and pretty. So, by simply experimenting with how early to turn off the blender and with what paper or papers to recycle, hundreds of different decorative and art sheets can be made.

Trying It.

Step 1. Get paper napkins of three or four different colors.

Step 2. Tear up enough of the above to make a single new sheet (enough to cover an area about seven inches square).

Step 3. Put the torn-up napkin pieces into water in a blender.

Step 4. Run the blender only four seconds.

Step 5. Make a sheet of paper as described in Chapter 2.

More Experiments

1. For later sheets, run the blender for different lengths of time.

2. Try recycling single sheets on which there are many different colors of ink.

3. Try recycling pieces of two or more papers of different colors at the same time.

4. Try tearing up the paper into smaller or larger pieces, or into both small and large pieces.

5. Recycle a sheet printed with words. Turn the blender off early. See whether single letters and/or whole words appear on the surface of your new sheet.

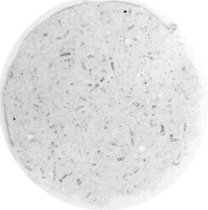

Try recycling these papers for mottled new sheets:

- Sunday colored comics

- V-8 Juice labels

- other colorful labels from food cans or jars

- used Christmas wrap

- any paper bearing many different colors of ink.

Chapter Four

Surface Embedment Technique

Discussion. Anything that is thin, flat and flexible, can be "locked on" to the surface of a sheet of handmade paper by the top layers of fibers. Even the thinnest sheet of paper is made up of numerous layers of the small papermaking fibers. Suitable materials can be put down into the last water and fibers descending toward the papermaking screen. The final fibers will "tie" the material into and onto the sheet's surface. Examples of suitable items include leaves, pieces of cloth, images cut out of newspapers, foliage such as arbor vitae, etc.

Trying It.

Step 1. Prepare pulp by running paper in a blender. Run the blender until few or no chunks of paper are left.

Step 2. Pour half the pulp into each of two containers. Add a half-cup of water to each container of pulp.

Step 3.

Cut out your favorite comic character (© Charlie Brown, © Garfield, © Cathy, © Doonesbury, etc.)* from the daily or Sunday comics.

*Are copyrighted.Peanuts, United Features Syndicate, Inc., Schultz; Garfield, United Features Syndicate, Inc., Jim Davis. Cathy, Universal Press Syndicate, Cathy Guisewite: Doonesbury, Universal Press Syndicate, G.B. Traudeau.

Step 4. Dip the cut-out into one of the containers of pulp. (This will make it wet and possibly will deposit a few papermaking fibers on the cut-out's edges.)

Step 5. With your tin cans set up for making paper, drape the wet cut-out over the rim of the top can.

Note: **The cut-out must be placed somewhere or in some manner that it can be quickly and easily picked up.**

Step 6. Start the papermaking process by dumping both containers of pulp into the top can.

Step 7. Immediately grab the cut-out, and, as the last water and fibers descend toward the screen, firmly push the cut-out down below the surface of the still-draining water, and onto the fibers already lying on the screen. The remaining fibers should descend and "tie" the embedded item into the sheet's surface.

Note: **Some pulps drain more rapidly than others. For surface embedment, recycle paper that results in a slower draining pulp, or add more water. Also, use a bit more pulp, because surface embedment is better on a somewhat thicker sheet. Greeting card thickness is good.**

Note: **Cutting off half the top tin can, or finding a shorter one, will make it easier to reach down. But be sure to tape any cut edge to prevent injury.**

Step 8. Continue with *Step 12* of the papermaking process as given in *Chapter 2,* and complete making your new sheet.

Other items to try with embedment:

- colorful fall leaf

- piece of colorful cloth

- piece of arbor vitae

- anything cut from newspaper or magazine

- larger piece of gold or silver foil

- flower petals or leaves

- anything thin, flat, and flexible that strikes your fancy.

Chapter Five

Internal Embedment Technique

Discussion. A sheet of paper is made up of little individual fibers. A variety of things can be mixed with the fibers and made a part of the sheet. These non-fiber additions, like colorful threads, can make the sheet beautiful and distinctive. But do not add too much non-fiber material, or the papermaking fiber's ability to keep the sheet together will be destroyed. Materials can be added to the fibers either in the blender when paper is being recycled into pulp, or, in the two containers of pulp just prior to pouring the pulp into the top can. Foliage, like leaves, thrown into the blender will shred into small bits and pieces. It's best not to add string or threads in the blender. They tend to wrap around the blender blades. Experience will show the best place to add specific materials.

Trying It.

(In this sheet, materials for embedment will be added after paper has been run in a blender.)

Step 1. Run paper in a blender to make pulp.

Step 2. Pour half the pulp into each of two containers.

Step 3. Add six or seven short pieces of different colored threads to each container.

Step 4. Stir the threads into the pulp.

Step 5. Form a new sheet of paper according to the directions given in *Chapter 2,* starting with *Step 11.*

Note: **Threads and other materials tend to migrate toward the sides of the top tin can (deckle). Watch for this. Use something like a plastic kitchen scraper to keep threads away from the top can's sides as the water drains.**

Try the following for additional sheets:

Sheet A. Place one or two dried leaves of trees or flowers into the blender with the paper to be recycled. It there are tree leaves, use the stems also.

Green leaves can be tried, but often this results in a greenish tinge around the foliage pieces in the final sheet.

Sheet B. Combine threads, ribbon lengths, leaves, grass from your lawn, in a single new sheet. Put leaves and grass into the blender with paper to be recycled. Add the threads to the pulp when it is in containers just before pouring.

Note: **Ribbon and thread tend to float. They might need to be pushed down below the surface of the draining water in order to be made secure in the new sheet.**

Sheet C. Try glitter. Add it either in the blender and/or in the containers just before pouring.

Try adding:

- shredded rope or twine

- bits of colored foil

- bits of colored
  strings

- shredded bark

- anything you think
  might work.

Chapter Six

Pulp Layering Technique

Discussion. Just as single fibers will bond to single fibers in the presence of water, batches of fibers bond to other batches of fiber if enough water is present. This means that you can make a sheet, remove no water from it, make a second sheet of a different color, shape, or size, remove no water from it either, and put it down as a "layer" on the surface of the first sheet. If the two layers are then handled as a single sheet for de-watering, pressing and drying, they will in fact be a single sheet at the end of the process.

There can be as many layers as the papermaker can handle. But water must always be present. Remember — remove no water before all layers are in place. Pulp layering opens broad horizons of art and decorative expression, especially in association with recycling which provides endless types and colors of pulp, free and instantly.

Trying It.

Pre-step information: For this technique, you will make two separate sheets. One will be smaller than the other. To make the smaller one, you will need a smaller tin can, both ends cut out, to use as the top can of your tin can hand mold. We would suggest a soup can that holds 10 ounces or so, or a vegetable can holding up to 17 ounces. Also, you will be making the second sheet before the first sheet is taken off the papermaking screen. So have another 6X6-inch piece of window screen ready on which to form the second sheet.

Step 1. Recycle paper of a single color into pulp with a blender. Make a sheet of paper as described in *Steps 1-4,* and *9-13,* in *Chapter 2.*

Step 2. Lift the new sheet and the papermaking screen straight up off the support screen and place them down on a surface. Do not remove any water from the new sheet.

Step 3. Recycle paper of a different color into pulp with your blender.

Note: **This pulp will be used to make the second sheet, which is much smaller. So you will need much less pulp. Put into the blender just a bit more paper (torn up) than it takes to cover the open end of the top can.**

Step 4.

Set up the hand mold with the smaller top can. Make a second sheet following the steps in *Step 1* above.

Step 5.

You are now ready to "layer" this second new sheet onto the surface of the first new sheet. Lift the papermaking screen and new sheet off the support screen.

Step 6.

While holding the second new sheet on its screen in mid-air, turn them over (so that the papermaking screen is on top, and the new sheet is on the bottom). The new sheet will not fall off unless it is very thick.

Step 7.

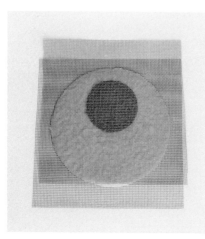

Lower the smaller new sheet carefully down onto the surface of the first, larger sheet. (You can place the smaller sheet wherever you wish on the larger sheet's surface.)

Step 8.

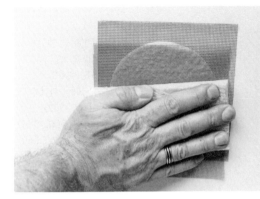

Press a sponge down firmly on the top papermaking screen. Wring water from the sponge and repeat pressing over the entire surface.

Step 9. Carefully lift the top papermaking screen. The smaller sheet should separate from the papermaking screen and stay bonded to the surface of the larger sheet.

Note: If the smaller sheet tends to rise with the screen, lay the screen back down and apply pressure again with the sponge. Some pulps tend to stick to the papermaking screen. If separation still fails to occur after more pressure has been applied, either try to peel the new sheet off, or, simply wash the sheet off the screen and make a new sheet with new pulp from a different type of paper.

Step 10. Continue with the regular papermaking process (*Step 18* in *Chapter 2*) just as though the two-layer sheet were a single sheet.

Discussion II. The second top tin can suggested above is round. However, different shapes can be layered on to the first sheet if different shaped cans can be found. For instance, a square can would layer a square shape. So keep an eye open for all types of containers (tin, plastic, etc.). Also look for cookie cutters which have high sides. In this way, a variety of shapes and sizes, as well as colors, can be layered onto a first sheet. More than one shape, if small enough, can be layered side-by-side onto the first sheet. A first sheet of a single monotone color can be made. Onto it can then be layered a smaller mottled sheet. This starts combining different techniques and opens the door to unlimited creativity.

Chapter Seven

The Pulp Gun

It's easy to make a pulp "gun." With it, you can "shoot" pulp onto a screen in a variety of shapes or abstract patterns.

You can shoot one color and then re-load and shoot another color. With good aim, you can form single or multicolor images such as numbers, letters, scenes or abstract patterns.

With the pulp layering technique, you can then place your numbers, letters, scenes or patterns on the surface of a regular sheet, making beautiful decorated paper or works of art.

Pulp guns can be made with any plastic "squeeze bottle" that has a lid which is a nozzle. Whenever the bottle is squeezed, whatever is inside shoots or oozes out through the nozzle.

Good for use as pulp guns are plastic squeeze bottles used for mustard and ketchup.

Trying It.

A. Make a sheet and leave it wet on the papermaking screen.

B. Recycle a different color of paper. Run the blender until there are no chunks left.

C. Pour the pulp into a plastic mustard or ketchup squeeze bottle. Fill the bottle half full.

D. Put the lid on. Be sure the nozzle is open.

E. Put a second papermaking screen on the support screen on the bottom tin can.

F. Take the pulp gun. Aim the nozzle down at the screen. Put the nozzle within two inches of the screen.

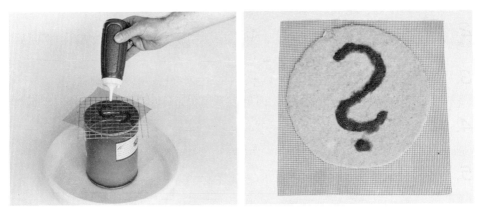

G. Give the plastic bottle a short, gentle squeeze. Later, try harder, longer squeezes.

H. Shoot (squeeze) little patches of pulp onto other places on the screen.

NOTE: **Do not pile up pulp in high ridges or mounds. Put down thin little patches, patterns and lines. Adding water to the pulp in the bottle will help keep pulp from getting too thick on the screen. Later you can experiment with thicker and thinner pulp in the bottle.**

I. Pick up the screen onto which you have "shot" pulp and pulp-layer it onto the sheet you made and left wet on the screen (see *Chapter 6, Step 5*).

J. Press and dry the sheet.

Congratulations — you have now made a work of art!

HOW TO EXPERIMENT WITH YOUR PULP GUN

1. Use thick and thinner pulps in the bottle.

2. Use different types of plastic bottles with larger or smaller nozzle openings.

3. Hold the bottle at different angles to the screen. At the same time, try squeezing harder and softer.

4. Try "writing" and "drawing" with the gun. Squirt pulp out into the form of your initials. Try shaping a tree.

5. Use two or more colors in the same "drawing" or abstract pattern.

You will find this so exciting, you will probably "shoot" until you are "shot".

Good luck and good recycling!

WHAT TO DO WITH ROUND PAPER

Chapter Eight

Rounding Things Out

A. Round paper lets you be different in letter writing.

   1. Write a round letter. Write your words in a circle. Or simply write words in lines as on regular sheets, but start and end the lines near the sheet's edges. This puts your words in a pleasing pattern.

2. Paste two sheets together with just a bit of one sheet overlapping the other. Fold one sheet over the other. Write your message on the inside. Put the address and stamp on the outside. Seal the two sheets together with a small piece of tape or with a decorative self-adhesive seal.

3. Write an illustrated letter. Divide the round sheet in half with a real or imaginary line up and down the middle. On the left-hand side, put a decoration or illustration. On the right-hand side, put your message.

The illustration can be
   a. your own drawing
   b. a friend's drawing
   c. a pasted in
      1. comic character cut-out
      2. other cut-out (from magazine, newspaper, Christmas card, etc.)
      3. leaf or other foliage
      4. photo
      5. seal or stamp
      6. anything that is flat.

4. Divide the sheet between top and bottom (instead of between sides) and do any of the things listed above. With this division, you will have different proportioned areas for your decoration or illustration.

5. Make a non-illustrated greeting card. Divide the sheet in halves. On one half, print a greeting for the occasion (Happy Birthday, Happy Anniversary, etc.). On the other side, write a short message. See illustration. Or, again, divide the sheet into top and bottom rather than into sides.

A. Use the sheet as a doily or coaster.

    1. For dry items, use as is.
    2. For wet items, sheet can be laminated between film (most printing shops can do laminations).

B. Create an Oriental type of "accordion" book. Paste three or more sheets together with the sheets slightly overlapping. See illustration on next page. Fold them in an accordion fold, creating pages. Write a letter, a poem of several verses, or make it an elaborate greeting card with message and illustrations and decorations on different pages.

It's bound to impress the person who receives it. Or keep it as part of your own "things to keep."

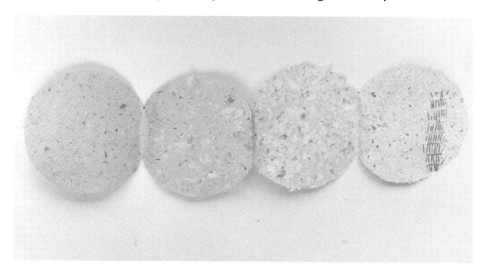

C. When you think a sheet is worthy, frame it in a round frame for your wall, or for giving as a present.

D. Embed leaves in a number of sheets for a "leaf" exhibit (or for a science class project). It can be an exhibit of

1. leaves from each of the trees on your lawn
2. leaves from a certain park, your school lawn, your city, your State's Capitol grounds, the Capitol grounds in Washington, D.C. Put the entire collection in a single frame.

E. Do D above, but instead of leaves, make a collection of:

1. comic strip characters
2. pictures cut from newspapers, magazines, etc., of
   a. friends and acquaintances
   b. birds or animals
   c. car accidents for a safety campaign for your school, city, church, etc.

d. small scenic views
e. sports "action" shots
f. any other "theme" that interests you.
3. Instead of framing the above, use each as the cover of a two-sheet greeting card described in A-2 above.

F. Make a special greeting card that is closed and opened with a ribbon. This can be done as follows.

1. Make a coffee can-size sheet. Leave it wet on the screen.
2. Lay a ribbon across the sheet down the middle. The ribbon should extend two to three inches past each edge of the sheet. See illustration.

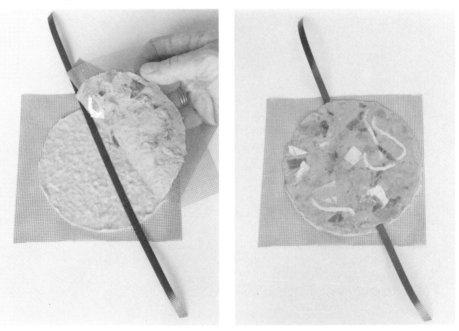

3. Make a second sheet and pulp-layer it over the ribbon onto the first sheet.
4. Press and dry.
5. Fold the sheet so that the two ribbon ends meet. Tie the "greeting card" shut with a bow in the ribbons.

*H.*Make a mobile of several sheets. Some or all of them can be decorated with surface embedments of leaves, etc., or with pulp layering designs, or use mottled sheets.

I. Make smaller sheets that can be used as "to" and "from" tags for birthday and Christmas gifts. The handmade tags will make the gifts mean more.

J. Make a small book. Staple a number of sheets together. Or try pasting. Or punch two holes near the edge of each sheet and use ribbon, yarn or decorative string to bind the sheets together. Or find a person or class from which you can learn about bookbinding. Libraries have books on the subject. Try one of the simpler binding techniques. Bookbinding is a good companion interest to papermaking. (Hand your teacher a "theme" on your own handmade paper which you yourself have bound together — that should do something.)

*K.*Make sheets for 100% recycled handmade invitations to parties or other affairs. Send them in envelopes you have made by hand from waste paper. *(See following chapter.)*

Many more ideas will occur to you as you work with recycling and handmade paper. It is a lot of fun and it gets your brain to working.

Chapter Nine

How To Recycle Sheets of Waste Paper Into Envelopes for Round Paper

By putting an envelope pattern over any printed or plain paper, tracing around it, cutting along the traced lines and then folding and pasting the cut out piece, you can create a new envelope that keeps all the beauty of color and image that was on the waste sheet you chose. It is quite easy. With all of the printed sheets in the world, you have a great selection for making envelopes.

Where do you get an envelope pattern? There are two places. One is taking an envelope you like and pulling it apart at the places it is glued together. Lay the dismantled envelope flat. Trace around it onto a piece of waste paper.

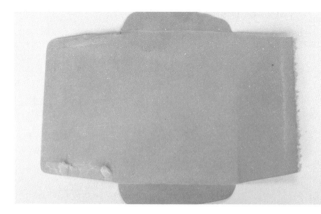

Or you can use the envelope pattern printed below. With a copy machine that enlarges, blow up the pattern below to the size you need for the round paper you make.

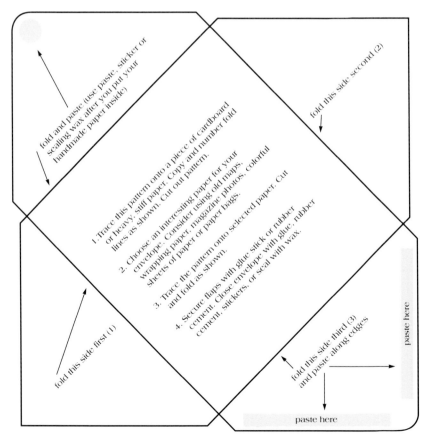

fold and paste (use paste, sticker or sealing wax after you put your handmade paper inside)

fold this side second (2)

1. Trace this pattern onto a piece of cardboard or heavy, stiff paper. Copy and number fold lines as shown. Cut out pattern.

2. Choose an interesting paper for your envelope. Consider using old maps, wrapping paper, magazine photos, colorful sheets of paper or paper bags.

3. Trace the pattern onto selected paper. Cut and fold as shown.

4. Secure flaps with glue stick or rubber cement. Close envelope with glue, rubber cement, stickers, or seal with wax.

fold this side first (1)

fold this side third (3) and paste along edges

paste here

paste here

When you have the pattern, do the following.

A. Lay the pattern down on the waste paper you have selected. Trace the pattern onto the sheet.

B. Lift off the pattern. Cut along the traced lines, cutting the pattern out of the waste sheet. What you have cut out, will become your envelope.

C. Fold the parts of your cut-out pattern by looking at the envelope you took apart. If you are using the pattern on page 60, reproduce at 195% on a copier and follow the directions given.

Note: **If you lay your pattern over a beautiful picture, the picture will become a part of your envelope.**

You have now found another way to recycle paper around your house into a useful, new product.

MORE INFORMATION ABOUT PAPER AND RECYCLING

Chapter Ten

Recycling...
New For People
Old For Paper

Recycling is a great idea. It can save the earth from being
filled with garbage.

MARKETPLACE *Magazine*

May, 1990
Volume 1, Number 8

Marketplace focus:
Personal finance

Recycling boom
offers business
opportunities

RECYCLE MICHAEL

APPLETON
RECYCLES

Karen Johnson
and her creation,
Recycle Michael

Parental leave: b
burner or hot iss

*Hayes Manufactu
family success ou
dim beginning*

Private 'courts' a faste
cheaper alternative

One of the most obvious recycling successes is the aluminum can. People and organizations everywhere are collecting them and selling them back to the manufacturer.

Sometimes the recycling process for a product is so complicated and expensive that recycling will not occur. In that case, people and society have to make a judgement. Either the product will be used and then buried in the earth when worn out, or, the product will not be used and will disappear from the market place, or, some modification will be made so that the product can be used and then recycled.

Probably no current product has been recycled longer than has paper. Paper has been recycled for over fourteen centuries. Evidence indicates that the Chinese, who invented it, recycled paper in the 4th and 5th Centuries.

Paper recycling, to varying degrees, has continued ever since. It probably increased when ever a shortage of raw materials occurred. It probably decreased when raw materials were plentiful and inexpensive.

In fact, in the Western world from the 12th to the mid-19th Centuries, all paper made, was made with recycled fibers. The respected cotton and linen rag papers of old were 100% recycled cotton and/or linen rags.

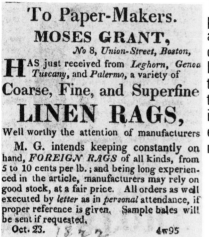

To Paper-Makers.

MOSES GRANT,

No 8, Union-Street, Boston,

HAS just received from *Leghorn, Genoa Tuscany,* and *Palermo,* a variety of

Coarse, Fine, and Superfine

LINEN RAGS,

Well worthy the attention of manufacturers

M. G. intends keeping constantly on hand, *FOREIGN RAGS* of all kinds, from 5 to 10 cents per lb. ; and being long experienced in the article, manufacturers may rely on good stock, at a fair price. All orders as well executed by *letter* as in *personal* attendance, if proper reference is given. Sample bales will be sent if requested.

Oct. 23.   4w95

The rags were purchased by the papermakers who, by mechanical action, literally beat the rags back down to the individual cotton or linen fibers which made up the threads which, in turn, made up the cloth. There is no other industry which has a record of existing so long on 100% recycling.

Today the paper industry is turning massively to recycling its own product. It might not be primarily because of any shortage of new (mostly tree) fibers, but because of social pressures in the market place.

Because paper might be the easiest of all products to recycle,

recycling is a bonanza for the hand papermaker. It makes almost every type of pulp made, plus what is added after the pulp has become paper, instantly available, free, for the mere turning on of a blender.

Considering the wide variety of pulps made, and how complex and expensive they can be in final form, their availability to any six-year-old who can turn on a blender with parental permission, is hardly believable. Then, with a couple tin cans and the decorative techniques described in this book, the six-year old can use the world's most expensive pulps to create art. No other industry has a product equally obliging (try recycling an aluminum can at home). As people find out about the ease of paper recycling, the craft and art of hand papermaking will grow by leaps and bounds. Whet your own appetite by exploring a free treasure house of fabulous fibers. It's the subject of *Chapter 13.*

Chapter Eleven

What Paper Is

Earlier chapters show that paper is not poured out in a continuous hard layer like cement.

Paper is a flat, even bundle of single fibers, which the papermaker must get as single fibers and put down as single fibers into a thin, even mat.

What is a fiber? It is a unit so tiny that seeing it without magnification is difficult. A "middle-size" fiber might be a little less than an eighth of an inch long and between one- and two-thousandths of an inch in diameter.

If you have very fine hair, and were to cut off a piece of hair three thirty-seconds of an inch long, you would have something like a papermaking fiber.

The fiber is wondrous. Scientists have studied it for years, but still have not learned everything about it.

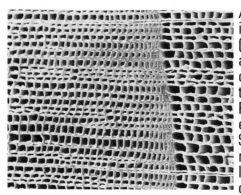

Among other things, the fiber is hollow like a drinking straw (as tiny as it is). So if we go to a tree stump and magnify the cut surface even a hundred times, we would see as in Figure 1, all the little open ended fibers lying side by side. So the mightiest tree is nothing more than millions of little fibers stacked beside and on top of each other.

Figure 1.

The papermaker, in an operation called "pulping", must get all the little fibers to come loose from each other so he can put them down as single fibers into a thin, even mat. That is not easy. The fibers hang together very strongly. For instance, go to a wooden table or chair and see if you can pull off a piece.

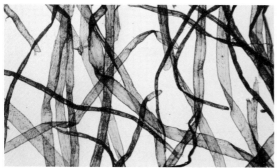

But the papermaker has learned to separate the fibers either with a grind stone, or with chemicals, or both.

When he has done that, he can float the fibers within water. The fibers can be seen in water in Figure 2.

Figure 2.

By having them in water, the papermaker can control the fibers.

They will go where the water goes. If he keeps them separated in water as in Figure 2, and then pours the water onto a sieve with a rim around it, the water will run through the sieve, and the fibers will be caught one by one on the sieve's surface.

That is how a papermaker puts millions of little fibers down one by one into a thin mat. Even the thinnest paper is made up of several layers.

Because of science's great instruments, we can see this. Figure 3 shows the surface and edge of a paper sheet magnified. There it can be seen that we do indeed write, draw or type on individual fibers when using paper. If you look closely with your own magnifying glass, you can probably count seven or eight layers of fibers that make up the thin sheet.

Figure 3.

One other way to show that paper is fibers is to show a magnified edge of paper all by itself. This is called a "cross section".

Figure 4 is a cross section of a piece of paper. You can see individual fibers. Most fibers collapse and become flat when made into paper. Some fibers here have kept their hollow center.

Figure 4.

Look closely to see a continuous black line on top of the fibers. That is ink! You are looking at the magnified cut edge of a sheet from a Chicago telephone directory, and the ink is likely a part of a letter or number in someone's name, address, or telephone number.

So you are now reading from a huge batch of little single fibers laid down in mats. Across the fibers' backs we have put ink in certain patterns. Behold, you and I can communicate!

Therefore, we hail the fabulous fiber. It has provided humanity a pocket in which all knowledge can be kept and, by copies, sent to the ends of the earth. In this sense, paper has created man's greatest scientific tools and allowed their use by people other than the inventors. It has captured wisdom and whimsy, prose and poetry, fact and fiction.

What more could one ask of a little chunk of cellulose an eighth of an inch long and a thousandth of an inch in diameter?

Chapter Twelve

Why Paper Can Be Recycled

Paper can be recycled because it is held together by a natural bond which anyone can create or destroy with water. Paper is a batch of individual fibers. The fibers are held together by a natural bond which develops at each spot where one fiber touches another *WHEN THEY MEET IN WATER.*

The fibers, though, must be *cellulose fibers*. Cellulose fibers are produced by all growing plants. They have been described as the most abundant material on the surface of the earth. The natural bond first occurs as the fibers touch in water. At that moment, it is so weak it cannot be measured. But as water is *taken away*, the bond gets stronger. In fact, it is a direct ratio — the bond's strength grows in direct proportion to the amount of water removed.

Consequently, the more water removed, the stronger each fiber holds on to the others which touch it. The strength of this natural bond is important because it is, to all extents and purposes, the strength of the paper. The bonding force is a miracle, but real. For recycling, the following is extremely important to note: if the strength of the bond *increases* as water is *removed*, the reverse is equally true — the strength of the bond decreases as water is *added*.

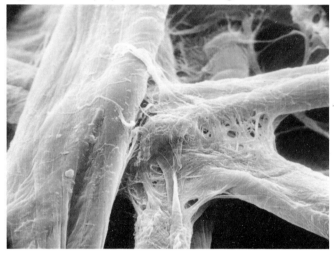

Bonded area in filter paper (magnification 1500X)

So that explains it. Paper is a batch of individual fibers held together by a natural bond existing wherever the fibers touch. When a batch of fibers has been used as paper, it isn't necessary to throw them away. Simply put the paper in water. That weakens the bond between fibers. Add mechanical agitation of the water, and the fibers will be separated, creating a mixture of individual fibers in water, which is "pulp". And it is from pulp that new paper is made.

Chapter Thirteen

A Free Treasure of Fibers

Paper is seldom just fibers. A paper mill almost always adds something to the fibers when preparing pulp. Things might be added before the pulp gets to the paper machine, or, things might be added on the paper machine as the pulp is becoming paper. Converters, who buy paper from paper mills, might add something to the paper while converting it to specific paper products. Consequently, paper is almost always fibers plus other materials.

A List of Papermaking Chemicals

Chemical	Major Applications (Pulping / Bleaching / Paper and paperboard)			Estimated Consumption Level (see Key #)

The "other materials" are why some papers are used for printing and others are used for wrapping hamburger at butcher shops. These "other materials" can be called "additives". Additives are used to make paper brighter, bulkier, water-resistant, fire retardant, etc. In the past, they have been used to make paper "medicinal". Additives represent power and variation.

Additives number in the many hundreds. Their combinations number in the thousands. In the single area of sizing (which is added to prevent liquid ink from feathering), papermakers might use corn starch, potato starch, tapioca starch, in either natural or chemically altered forms. Or they might use one of a variety of synthetic sizings. Animal glue, used historically, is probably still available. Extracts of most any root or plant provides sizing to some degree.

Dyes might be added to produce colored pulps for making colored papers. Each additive costs money to buy and money and time to insert into the pulp. Money is required for necessary equipment to handle the additives. Their successful use requires knowledge and, frequently, experience.

BUT THE HAND PAPERMAKER WHO RECYCLES GETS ALL OF THE ABOVE FREE, IN ABOUT THIRTY SECONDS. THIS INCLUDES THE FIBERS (REFINED OR UNREFINED), ADDITIVES, COST OF EQUIPMENT, COST OF SALARIES OF PROFESSIONAL AND SCIENTIFIC PERSONNEL REQUIRED TO ASSEMBLE THE PULP, AND TIME. COST TO THE RECYCLING PAPERMAKER — A CUP OF WATER, USE OF A BLENDER, AND ABOUT THIRTY SECONDS WORTH OF ELECTRICITY.

The hundreds of specialized additives — for bulk, color, brightness, water resistance, etc., and all other specialized ingredients, are free to the recycling papermaker, as are wax coated or impregnated papers for food wraps, and thousands of pulps containing thousands of combinations of additives, each of which will provide a different kind of new paper.

The possibilities are beyond counting. For the hand papermaker, recycling opens a whole world of investigation, discovery, experimentation and adventure. The numbers and kinds of pulps in the form of different types of papers that enter any hand papermaker's life in a single week, is unbelievable.

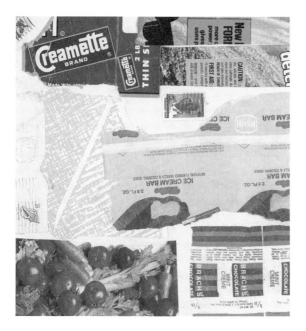

They will come in the mailbox as newspapers, magazines, junk mail, coupons, personal correspondence, and more; from grocery stores as sales flyers, sales slips, labels on many different bottles and cans, specialized packaging; from concerts, plays, and other entertainment, as programs for those events. More papers will come as books, pamphlets, and other publications.

Thus, for wild, tame, exotic, standard, exciting, dull, single or multicolored new papers with an array of varied tactile and visual textures, recycling presents the hand papermaker a never-emptying bin of quality pulp, free.

The secret to effective use of the vast and free fiber treasure is to experiment, to be curious, to recycle a sample of absolutely every piece of paper ever to enter the papermaker's purview. Nothing should be permitted to escape, no matter how odd, how obscure, or how unlikely the paper might appear. Through this kind of total and saturation effort, the papermaker will begin to realize the endless potential of the free "treasure of fibers."

APPENDIX

PAPERMAKING INFORMATION AND EQUIPMENT

Available from

Greg Markim, Inc.
PO Box 13245
Milwaukee, WI 53213
Tel. 1-414-453-1480

- Tin Can Papermaking™ Kit
  packets of professional materials that
  complement this book
- Classroom Tin Can Papermaking™ Kit
- Clear Demonstration Cylinder
- Hand Papermaking Kits for 6"x8" sheets
- Hand Papermaking Kits for 8 1/2"x11" sheets
- Professional Papermaking Screens
- Professional Couch (laboratory blotter) sheets
- Hydraulic Jack Press frames
- Information and teaching materials,
  PAPERMAKING FOR EVERYONE, video
  PAPER BY KIDS, book
  TIN CAN PAPERMAKING™, book

Other Suppliers

Twinrocker, Inc.
P.O. Box 413
Brookston, IN. 47923

Lee McDonald, Inc.
P.O. Box 264
Charlestown, MA 02129

Carriage House Paper
1 Fitchburg Street #C-207
Somerville, MA 02143

THE AUTHOR

Arnold E. Grummer accumulated a vast store of paper knowledge during sixteen years as an editor and faculty member at the internationally known graduate school and research center, the former Institute of Paper Chemistry in Appleton, WI. He added historical knowledge during six years as Curator of the Dard Hunter Paper Museum, the world's major paper historical collection. He is the author of **Paper By Kids**, which has sold more than 20,000 copies. He has made a fifty-seven minute video, **Papermaking For Everyone**. He is the author of paper-related articles in an encyclopedia, a history reference book, and in magazines in the United States and abroad. He lectures and has done trade show and mall demonstrations in the United States and Canada. His museum appearances include the Smithsonian Institution in Washington D.C. and the Chicago Museum of Science and Industry. Besides the paper and printing industries, his professional audiences have included the FBI and the IRS. School audiences have ranged from elementary schools to college and university art departments. He does workshops for professional artists. With occasional help from son Greg, and daughter Kim Schiedermayer, he operates a private mill, the Quarter Moon Mill, which produces 100% recycled fiber handmade art cards. He markets his personally designed hand papermaking equipment and system through Greg Markim, Inc. He is author of a non-papermaking book, **The Great Balloon Game Book and More Balloon Activities.**

Credits

Book Design: Spencer D. Rotzel
Layout: Spencer D. Rotzel
Cover Design: Spencer D. Rotzel
Handmade Paper: Arnold E. Grummer
Production: Rotzel Graphic Design Studio
Photographs: Arnold E. Grummer and courtesy
    of the former Institute of Paper Chemistry
Typesetting: Spencer D. Rotzel
Fonts: Americana and Eurostile
Printing: Spectra Print Corp., Stevens Point, WI

Author with the late Dard Hunter, founder of Dard Hunter Museum.